# Incredible
# Creatures

## WELDON OWEN PTY LTD

**Chairman:** John Owen
**Publisher:** Sheena Coupe
**Associate Publisher:** Lynn Humphries
**Managing Editor:** Helen Bateman
**Design Concept:** Sue Rawkins
**Senior Designer:** Kylie Mulquin
**Production Manager:** Caroline Webber
**Production Assistant:** Kylie Lawson

**Text:** Robert Coupe
**Consultant:** George McKay, Conservation Biologist
**U.S. Editors:** Laura Cavaluzzo and Rebecca McEwen

09 08 07 06 05 04
12 11 10 9 8 7 6

Published in the United States by
**Wright Group/McGraw-Hill**
One Prudential Plaza
Chicago IL 60601
www.WrightGroup.com

Printed in Singapore.
ISBN: 0-7699-0466-1
ISBN: 0-7699-0589-7 (6-pack)

# CONTENTS

**Reaching Up and Out**
Most long-necked dinosaurs, called sauropods, ate leaves and plants.

# FROM THE PAST

Crocodiles and lizards are reptiles. Dinosaurs were reptiles, too. The first dinosaurs lived more than 220 million years ago. The last ones died out about 65 million years ago. Some were huge. Others were as small as chickens.

**Plants or Meat?**
Some dinosaurs, such as the huge Apatosaurus, ate only plants. Others, such as Ornitholestes, lived on animal flesh.

# ODD AND UGLY

People have dreamed up some strange-looking animals and made up incredible stories, or myths, about them. Some real animals look strange to us, too. Many of them also behave in unusual ways. The odd-looking animals on these pages all live under the sea.

**Single File**
Every year in fall, spiny lobsters walk across the ocean floor in long lines like the one you see here.

## Long and Pointy

A unicorn was a mythical horse that had a single horn on its head. The unicorn fish is named after it.

## Colorful but Dangerous

Stonefish live in parts of the Pacific Ocean. The spines on their back are full of poison.

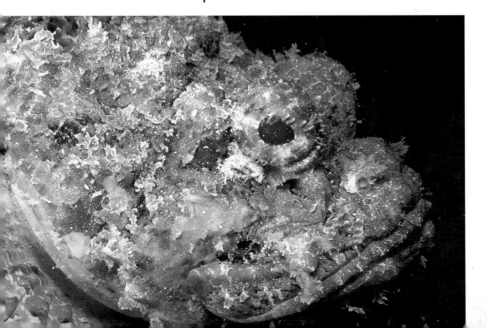

# CREEPY CRAWLY

Spiders eat other animals. Most feed on insects. Spiders get eaten, too. Birds, lizards, frogs, and stinging insects hunt them. The trapdoor spider burrows in the ground. When a hunting wasp comes after it, the spider goes into its hole head first. The back of its body is too thick for the wasp to sting.

### Hiding and Squirting

A puss moth can pull its head into its body so an enemy can't see it. It can also squirt acid from its throat.

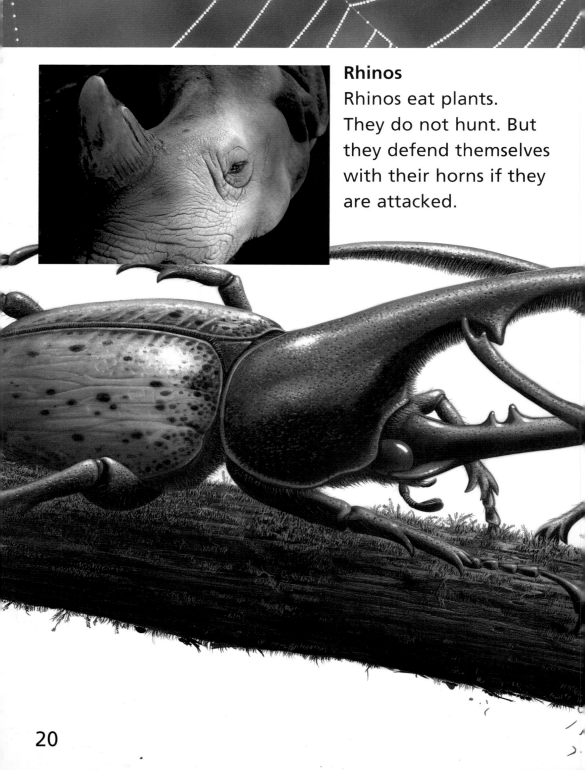

### Rhinos

Rhinos eat plants.
They do not hunt. But
they defend themselves
with their horns if they
are attacked.

# TUSKS AND HORNS

Some large animals have tusks, horns, or antlers. They are useful when these animals fight or defend themselves. There is also a beetle that fights with horns. It is called the hercules beetle. In the picture below, two male beetles fight about a female. She is the one with no horns.

**Toothy Tusks**
The walrus uses its long tusks to pull itself out of the water.

## Humming Feathers

When a racket-tailed drongo flies, its tail feathers make a humming sound.

## Crowning Glory

Crowned cranes have crests like golden crowns on their head.

# GROWING ANTLERS

Like plants, deer's antlers start growing in spring. They are fully grown in summer. They start to wither in fall, and they fall off in winter. Next spring, they grow again.

1. Early spring

2. Late summer

3. Fall

4. Winter

# FANCY FEATHERS

Birds are the only animals that have feathers, and the feathers of many birds are bright and colorful. Some birds have feathers in strange and interesting shapes. A few male birds, such as peacocks and lyre birds, can spread out their long tail until it looks like an enormous fan. Their tail is so long, it makes it hard for the birds to fly.

**Fantail**
A male peacock has
more than 200 huge tail feathers.

# CATCH A RIDE

When a baby kangaroo is born, it is tiny and weak, so its mother keeps it in a special pouch. The baby drinks milk from nipples inside the pouch. After about seven months, it comes out for the first time. For a year or so, however, it lives mainly in the pouch, where it is safe and warm. Animals that keep their young in pouches are called marsupials. Koalas are marsupials. So are possums.

# DID YOU KNOW?

Just as humans are right or left handed, elephants are right or left tusked. The tusk they use most is usually shorter.

## INSIDE AND OUT

A young kangaroo, or joey, climbs into the pouch head first. It then pulls its body in until its head is at the front. It twists itself around so that it can see out. It is now ready to jump out again when it needs food or exercise.

**Vampire Bat**
There is a group of bats called leaf-nosed bats. The vampire bat is one of them.

# FUNNY FACES

When you think of someone you know, it is probably their face that you see in your mind. If you came face to face with any of the animals on these pages, you would find them hard to forget. One thing these animals have in common is that they are all mammals. Another is their weird and wonderful, but very different, faces.

## Pot-bellied Pig

The Vietnamese pot-bellied pig has tiny, beady eyes in its large, round face.

## Mandrill

A mandrill is an African monkey. This is a male. Females' faces are not as colorful.

Here are some more strange faces, from different parts of the animal kingdom. Two are mammals. The tapir is a hoofed animal, and the tarsier is a mammal that lives in trees. The manta ray is a fish that swims in many of the world's oceans, and the ruff is a wading bird that lives near coasts and the shores of lakes and rivers.

**Tapir**
A tapir has a long, thin snout. At the end, there is a short trunk that can move around like an elephant's trunk.

## Ruff

This is how a male ruff looks every spring, when it grows a mass of loose feathers around its face and neck.

## Tarsier

The tarsier's huge staring eyes help it to see at night, when it hunts for its food.

## Manta Ray

A manta ray looks fierce and frightening as it swims along with its huge mouth wide open.

# GLOSSARY

**crest** Feathers that stick up on the top of some birds' heads.

**iguanas** Large lizards that often have spines on their head and back.

**mammal** An animal that grows inside its mother's body before it is born. The young drink their mother's milk.

**pangolin** A toothless mammal from Asia and Africa that is covered with horny scales.

**reptiles** Cold-blooded animals that have backbones and dry skin covered by scales or a hard shell.

# INDEX

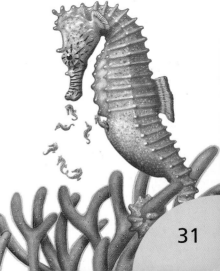

# CREDITS AND NOTES

**Picture and Illustration Credits**

[t=top, b=bottom, l=left, r=right, c=center, F=front, B=back, C=cover, bg=background]

**Corel Corporation** 3t, 6br, 7tc, 15tr, 15bc, 17rc, 18rc, 19br, 20tl, 21tr, 23c, 27bl, 27tr, 29cl, 28bl, 30t, 4–32 borders, Cbg. **Simone End** 25rc, BC. **Christer Eriksson** 12bl, 13c, 19–22c, 31br, FCc. **FLPA** 28tr. **John Francis/Bernard Thornton Artists UK** 5tc, 6cl. **Robert Hynes** 8–9bl, 8c. **David Kirshner** 1c, 2l, 7bc, 18l, 26tl, 29r, FCbr. **John Mac/FOLIO** 11c, 22c, 24–25c. **James McKinnon** 4bl, 4tc, 16–17rc, FCt. **John Richards** 10tr. **Andrew Robinson/illustration** 5br. **Trevor Ruth** 14l, 16tr. **Tom Stack and Associates** 9cr.

**Acknowledgements**

Weldon Owen would like to thank the following people for their assistance in the production of this book: Jocelyne Best, Peta Gorman, Tracey Jackson, Andrew Kelly, Sarah Mattern, Emily Wood.